10-Minute F

I0018281

OS X Mountain Lion
New Features

Chris Kennedy

Excerpted from
OS X Mountain Lion (Tech 102)

Questing Vole Press

OS X Mountain Lion New Features (10-Minute Fixes)
by Chris Kennedy

Editor: Bill Gregory
Proofreader: Pat Kissell
Compositor: Birgitte Lund
Cover Illustrator: Rayne Beaudoin
Cover: Questing Vole Press

Version 10.82.0

Contents

OS X Mountain Lion
New Features

Most of Mountain Lion's big-ticket new features make your Mac more iPad-like. You'll find OS X versions of Notification Center, Dictation, Game Center, Messages, Notes, Reminders, and more. These features aren't copied exactly from iPad—Apple has adapted them to work on mouse-and-menu-driven Macs rather than on finger-driven touchscreens. iCloud enhancements let you share your documents, contacts, appointments, and other content across your Mac, Windows PC, and iOS devices (iPad, iPhone, and iPod touch).

Not all the big changes are iPad-related. The new Gatekeeper feature, for example, restricts which downloaded apps can be installed, protecting your Mac from viruses, spyware, and other malware. And AirPlay Mirroring mirrors (duplicates) whatever is on your Mac's screen to a high-definition TV (HDTV) via Apple TV. A few apps have been renamed or replaced: iChat is now Messages, Address Book is now Contacts, and iCal is now Calendar.

This guide covers the major differences between Mountain Lion and its predecessor, Lion. For a complete look at Mountain Lion, see my book *OS X Mountain Lion (Tech 102)*.

Installing Mountain Lion

Unlike early (pre-Lion) versions of OS X, you can't get a copy of Mountain Lion on a DVD. Instead, you buy and download Mountain Lion from the Mac App Store ((> App Store). Mountain Lion is a large download (>4 GB); if you don't have a fast or reliable network connection, you can take your Mac to an Apple retail store (*apple.com/retail/storelist*) for help buying and installing Mountain Lion. You can install it on any Mac that meets the system requirements, listed at *apple.com/osx/specs*. The general requirements are:

- OS X 10.6.8 or later (that is, Snow Leopard or Lion)

- 2 GB of memory

- 8 GB of available space

Apple also lists which models support Mountain Lion:

- iMac (Mid 2007 or newer)

- MacBook (Late 2008 Aluminum, or Early 2009 or newer)

- MacBook Pro (Mid/Late 2007 or newer)

- Xserve (Early 2009)

- MacBook Air (Late 2008 or newer)

- Mac mini (Early 2009 or newer)

- Mac Pro (Early 2008 or newer)

Some new features, such as AirPlay Mirroring, require recent (2011 or newer) models. To determine whether your Mac qualifies, choose > About This Mac > More Info button. The Overview pane shows your model, release date, and memory (click Storage to check free space). You can install your copy of Mountain Lion on as many Macs as you own, without serial numbers or copy protection.

Tip: In Terminal, you can use the command **uname -a** to print details about your hardware and operating system.

Reinstalling Mountain Lion

Should the need arise, you can reinstall Mountain Lion without using a DVD or disk image. When you first install Mountain Lion, the installer silently creates a new partition on your hard drive that you can use to reinstall Mountain Lion. (Your existing data are safely preserved during repartition.) This stealth partition, named Recovery HD (or Recovery-10.8), is invisible in Finder and Disk Utility, but you can see it by using the `diskutil list` command in Terminal. To recover Mountain Lion, hold down the Option key during startup and then choose Recovery HD when the list of startup partitions appears. Alternatively, hold down Command+R during startup to boot directly to Recovery HD. You can also boot to Recovery HD from a locally connected Time Machine backup drive.

Tip: If FileVault is turned on, Recovery HD won't appear when you hold down the Option key during startup, but you can still hold down Command+R to boot directly to it.

Notification Center

Certain applications can push notifications to your Mac, even when you're not actively using the program. Notification Center is the central list of all the apps that are trying to get your attention. Apps that can send notifications include:

- Calendar for events and invitations.

- Reminders for reminders coming due.

- Game Center for friend requests and game invitations.

- Mac App Store for software updates.

- Mail for incoming email from all senders, only contacts, or only VIP senders.

- Messages for new messages.

- Safari for website alerts (websites must be open in Safari).

- FaceTime for missed calls.

- Twitter for direct messages and mentions (you can also tweet right to Twitter from Notification Center).

- Facebook for Facebook notifications (you can also post right to Facebook from Notification Center).

- Third-party apps whose developers tap into Notification Center.

When you receive a notification, a small floating window appears in the top-right corner of the screen, containing the notification. Notifications come in two forms: banners and alerts. A **banner** slides into view and then disappears after 5 seconds. An **alert** remains visible until you acknowledge it by clicking Close, Show, Snooze, or whatever. Clicking a banner opens the corresponding application to show the related item. (If you click a Mail subject heading, for example, Mail opens and displays that message.)

If a banner notification disappears before you can get to it, you can open Notification Center at any time (even from a full-screen app) to see a list of recent notifications.

When you open Notification Center, the desktop background shifts leftward to reveal all current notifications in a sorted list along the right edge of your screen.

To open Notification Center:

Do any of the following things:

- Click the Notification Center icon ≡ near the right edge of the menu bar. This icon (which you can't hide) turns blue when new notifications arrive.

- Flick two fingers from the right edge of the trackpad into the center (as if you were pulling something away from the right side of the screen). Accuracy counts: you must start to flick from the right edge.

- Press the Notification Center keyboard shortcut. To assign this shortcut, choose > System Preferences > Keyboard > Keyboard Shortcuts pane, click Mission Control (on the left), select Show Notification Center (or double-click it if it's already selected), and then hold down the new keys.

To close Notification Center without responding to a notification:

Do any of the following things:

- Click :≡.

- Flick two fingers to the right.

- Click anywhere off Notification Center.

To hide alerts and banners temporarily:

Do any of the following things:

- Hold down the Option key and then click :≡.

- Scroll to the top of Notification Center and then turn off "Show Alerts and Banners".

Only pop-up alerts and banners are hidden. Notifications still appear when you open Notification Center.

Tip: Alerts and banners are hidden automatically when you're presenting in Keynote, when your Mac is connected to a projector, or when your display is mirrored on an external monitor.

To configure Notification Center:

Choose > System Preferences > Notifications, or open Notification Center and then click the gear icon in the bottom-right corner.

Apps that can send notifications are listed on the left. Click an app to change its settings.

For each app, you can set:

- Whether an app sends notifications.

- Whether you receive banner or alert notifications (or none at all).

- The order in which notifications are listed (for manual sorting, drag apps up or down to reorder the list).

- How many recent notifications appear in Notification Center.

- Whether to display an alert badge (a number in a little red circle) on the notifying app's dock icon.

- Whether to play a sound as part of the notification.

Some applications let you set additional notification and alert options within the app itself (typically in the Preferences dialog box). In Mail, for example, choose Mail > Preferences > General pane > "New message notifications". In Safari, choose Safari > Preferences > Notifications pane.

Game Center

Use the Game Center application to play games on Apple's online multiplayer social gaming network, which Apple says has more than 100 million members around the world. You can get Game Center-compatible games from the Mac App Store to play against friends or strangers on iPhones, iPads, iPod touches, or Macs.

Tip: Chess (in the Applications folder) supports Game Center.

Game Center offers features common to most gaming networks:

- You can add people to your friends list or receive friend requests from others.

- Friends can invite each other to play or find equally matched opponents.

- You can earn bonus points for games that reward points for completing certain tasks, and you can see what your friends have achieved.

- Game leaderboards rank the best players.

- In-game voice chat lets you talk with your opponents or team members during multiplayer games.

Game Center supports parental controls, full-screen view, and notifications for friend requests and game invitations.

To use Game Center, you need an internet connection and an Apple ID. If you like, you can create a separate Apple ID for gaming and still use your main Apple ID for iCloud, App Store, iTunes, and so on.

The first time that you sign in to Game Center, you must create a **nickname**, which is your unique user name in Game Center. If you pick a nickname that someone is already using, Game Center suggests alternatives, which you're free to ignore. If you see your nickname at the top of the Me pane, you're already signed in. You can change your nickname at any time in account settings, but only one nickname at a time can be associated with an Apple ID. Other players can search for you by using your nickname. Account settings also let you configure privacy-related options, such as whether to accept game invitations or display your real name to nonfriends.

After you sign in, click the buttons in the toolbar to edit your account, play or buy games, or manage your friends:

Me
> View or buy top games; add or take a photo; declare your status, which you define; view or edit your account settings (Account banner > View Account); or sign out (Account banner > Sign Out).

Tip: You don't need to sign out each time you quit Game Center.

Friends
> Invite people or contacts to be friends; get friend recommendations; invite friends to play; see games that friends play; buy a game that a friend has; check a friend's scores; search your friends list; list a friend's friends; remove (unfriend) a friend; or report problems or cheaters.

Tip: No friends? Unresponsive friends? Click Auto-Match to have Game Center find another player for you.

Games
> Play a game; get game recommendations; search for Game Center games; tell a friend about a game; view leaderboards (rankings) and achievements; or get a game from the App Store. Not all Game Center-compatible games feature multiplayer play.

Tip: To find Game Center games from within App Store, open App Store (> App Store), click Categories (in the toolbar), and then click Games.

Challenges

Send or receive challenges to beat friends' scores or earn achievements.

Requests

Invite people to be friends; respond to friend requests; or search for requests.

Tip: Apple maintains and updates your Game Center **profile** automatically. Your profile contains your nickname, friends list, achievement points, photo, status, Game Center-compatible games owned, and more.

In many multiplayer games—racing and cooperative games being obvious examples—all players play at the same time. Other games—particularly board and card games such as backgammon, Scrabble, and poker—are **turn-based**, in that each player waits until the other acts before proceeding. Game Center keeps track of each player's turn and can manage multiple games if you're playing more than one. If it's taking a long time between moves, Game Center can send you notifications when it's your turn.

Dictation

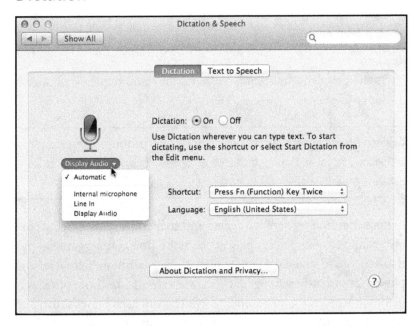

You can dictate text instead of typing on the keyboard. Dictation works with text areas in any OS X app; no additional third-party developer support is required. To dictate, you must be connected to the internet. When you dictate text, what you say is sent to Apple to convert it to text. Other personal information (such as contact names) may be sent too. For details, click About Dictation and Privacy in the Dictation pane. Dictation supports parental controls.

To set up dictation:

Choose > System Preferences > Dictation & Speech > Dictation pane. In the Dictation pane, turn on Dictation. If you like, use the Shortcut pop-up menu to change the keyboard shortcut that triggers dictation (to create a shortcut that's not in the list, choose Customize and then press two or more keys you want to use). Choose your language and dialect from the Language pop-up menu. To dictate by using a specific microphone, click the pop-up menu below the microphone icon. No other special setup or voice training is required.

To dictate text:

Place the insertion point where you want the dictated text to appear (you can dictate text anywhere that you can type it—try practicing in Notes). Press the Fn key twice or choose Edit > Start Dictation. When the microphone icon appears, speak your text calmly (the icon glows to show your speaking volume). When you're done, press the Fn key or click the Done button. Your spoken text appears.

To enter punctuation, say the punctuation mark. Suppose that you want to dictate "Without me, you're nothing." Say this:

Without me comma you're nothing period

Here are some tips for using Dictation:

- To start a new paragraph, say "new paragraph". To insert a line break, say "new line".

- To type 5 rather than five, say "numeral five". Saying more than one digit in a row also produces numerals: saying "four five" types 45, not *four five*. Say "point" to insert a decimal point: "six point five" types 6.5.

- Currency amounts and dates are recognized automatically. "fourteen dollars and twenty five cents" types $14.25. "july twenty seventh twenty twelve at six thirty AM" types *July 27, 2012 at 6:30 AM*.

- Emoticons: "smiley" types :-). "frowny" types :-(. "winky" types ;-).

The more you use Dictation, the better it understands you. Unclear text is underlined in blue. If the text is wrong, click it and then select an alternate, or type or dictate the correct text. Make sure that the mic is unobstructed by hands, clothing, or other objects. If you dictate in a noisy or echo-prone place, it may help to use a headset microphone. If you use an external mic, set its input volume high enough to respond to your voice (choose > System Preferences > Sound > Input pane).

Tip: Dictation is integrated with Contacts. Say a contact's name, and Dictation knows who you mean and spells it correctly.

Gatekeeper

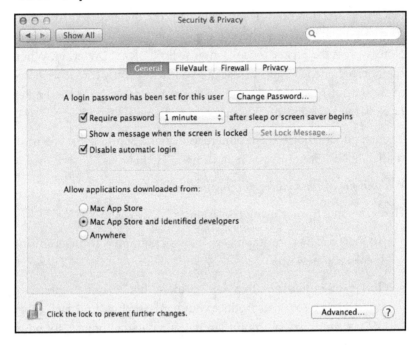

Gatekeeper is a security feature that helps prevent you from inadvertently installing viruses, spyware, and other malware (malicious software). Gatekeeper works by restricting which downloaded apps you can install.

To set up Gatekeeper:

Choose > System Preferences > Security & Privacy > General pane (click if the settings are dimmed).

Under "Allow applications downloaded from", choose one of the following options:

Mac App Store
> Download and run apps from only the Mac App Store. The App Store is the safest place to get apps because it's curated, meaning that Apple vets the developers and reviews their apps before accepting them to the store. If there's a problem with an app, Apple removes

it from the store. Before you download and install an app, you can read reviews from other users.

Mac App Store and identified developers

Download and run App Store apps and non-App Store apps that have a Developer ID. Developers that register with Apple get a unique Developer ID, which they can use to digitally sign the apps that they create. This digital signature is cryptographically secure and lets Gatekeeper verify that the app hasn't been tampered with since it left the hands of the developer. Signed apps aren't necessarily sold through the App Store and aren't pre-screened by Apple, but if Apple discovers any problems with apps created by a registered developer, they can block that developer's apps and revoke their credentials. OS X updates its list of blacklisted developers once each day.

Anywhere

Download and run apps from anywhere. Note that Apple charges a yearly fee for a Developer ID and takes a large cut (30%) of all apps sold through the App Store, so plenty of unregistered but legitimate developers avoid the "Apple tax" by selling their apps through their own websites and other non-Apple stores.

Gatekeeper works only the first time that you try to launch an app, and only when that app has been downloaded via a web browser, an email client, or a similar program (Gatekeeper doesn't check apps copied from USB or network drives). After an app has been launched once, it's beyond the reach of Gatekeeper.

Tip: To manually override your Gatekeeper setting, right-click an unsigned app in Finder and then choose Open.

Calendar

Use the Calendar application to manage your calendars and events (appointments). Calendar identifies you by your Apple ID (Calendar > Preferences > Accounts pane) and is integrated with Contacts. Calendar supports Auto Save and full-screen view.

Calendar includes these features:

- View individual calendars or multiple color-coded calendars at the same time (choose View > Show Calendar List or click Calendars in the toolbar).

- Add new events (File > New Event).

- Edit existing events (Edit > Edit Event).

- View and search recent and upcoming events.

- Enter repeating events (such as birthdays or weekly meetings).

- Specify what hours constitute a workday and what weekday starts the week (Calendar > Preferences > General pane).

- Receive onscreen, audio, email, or message alerts of upcoming events (Edit > Edit Event > Alert).

- Send notifications for events and invitations (Calendar > Preferences > Alerts pane).

- Create multiple calendars for home, work, and so on (File > New Calendar).

- Set the default calendar for new events (Calendar > Preferences > General pane > Default Calendar).

- Switch among daily (Command+1), weekly (Command+2), monthly (Command+3), and yearly (Command+4) views.

- Import, export, and print calendars (File menu).

- Use iCloud to sync your calendars across your Macs, Windows PCs, and iOS devices (Calendar > Preferences > Accounts pane > iCloud).

- To sync Calendar with Gmail, Yahoo, or other services that support calendars, choose ⌘ > System Preferences > Mail, Contacts & Calendars, select the account, and then turn on Calendars & Reminders.

Calendar also lets you view the online calendars of people who have published them on the internet. You can subscribe to **iCalendar** (.ics) or **CalDAV** calendars, including iCloud, Yahoo, Google, and Calendar for iOS calendars. You can read events from subscribed calendars, but you can't add or edit events. To subscribe to a calendar, choose File > New Calendar Subscription (Option+Command+S).

You can also subscribe to web calendars by clicking a link to the calendar in Safari. Open Safari, go to a site such as *icalshare.com*, find a calendar that you like (holidays, sports schedules, movie releases, and so on), and then click Subscribe to Calendar. The new calendar is added to your subscription list, and its events appear in Calendar. To show or hide those events, click the Calendars button in the toolbar and then toggle the target calendar.

To edit or delete a calendar subscription, right-click the calendar in the Calendars list.

If you get an iCalendar (.ics) file attached to an email message, you can open the attachment to import its events into Calendar.

Contacts

Use the Contacts application to store names, addresses, telephone numbers, email addresses, birthdays, and other contact information. Contacts supports Auto Save and share sheets.

Contacts includes these features:

- In its default view, Contacts resembles a physical address book. On the left page, browse contacts by clicking, scrolling, or searching. On the right page, scroll contact info, or click a field or button to perform an action such as sharing a contact or opening a contact's home page.

- To create a new contact, choose File > New Card (Command+N) or click ⊞. Your contacts are available in Mail, Messages, FaceTime, Calendar, file sharing, AirDrop, and other apps and services that tap into Contacts.

- To edit an existing contact, select the contact and then choose Edit > Edit Card (Command+L) or click the Edit button.

- To specify which fields appear in all cards, choose Contacts > Preferences (Command+,) > Template pane. To add a field to a specific card, select the card and then choose Card > Add Field.

- To change how contacts are sorted and displayed, choose Contacts > Preferences (Command+,) > General pane.

- To sync your contacts with iCloud, Yahoo, or other contact lists, choose Contacts > Preferences (Command+,) > Accounts pane. Alternatively, choose > System Preferences > Mail, Contacts & Calendars, select the account, and then turn on Contacts.

- To use iCloud to sync your contacts across your Macs, Windows PCs, and iOS devices, choose Contacts > Preferences (Command+,) > General pane > Default Account > iCloud. To store your contacts on only your Mac, choose On My Mac as the default account.

- Each Contacts entry is a customizable "card". You can use the File menu to import and export cards in common formats, organize them into fixed or self-updating ("smart") groups, or print contact lists and address labels.

- You can use the View menu to display groups (Command+1), lists and cards (Command+2), or only cards (Command+3).

- Contacts exchanges contact information with other programs (including Windows programs) mainly through **vCards** (.vcf files). If you get a vCard file attached to an email, drag the file into your Contacts window to create a contact. To create a vCard file, drag an entry (or Command-drag multiple entries) out of your Contacts list to the desktop or into an outgoing message. To change the vCard format, choose Contacts > Preferences (Command+,) > vCard pane.

- To control which apps and services can access your contacts, choose > System Preferences > Security & Privacy > Privacy pane > Contacts (click if necessary).

- Facebook friends appear in Contacts with profile photos and up-to-date information.

Messages

Use the Messages application for instant text messaging, audio/video chatting, and file exchange. Messages supports notifications and full-screen view.

In addition to supporting the ubiquitous SMS and MMS messaging services used on mobile phones and the web, Messages supports Apple's **iMessage** service. iMessage is a free alternative to SMS/MMS that lets you send unlimited free text messages, photos, videos, and more to people who are also running Messages on their iPads, iPhones, iPod touches, or Macs, and with whom you've exchanged email addresses. iMessage identifies you by your Apple ID email address and requires an internet connection. iMessages are displayed on all your Macs and iOS devices logged in to the same account. You can start a conversation on, say, your iPad and then continue it on your Mac. Set up Messages on each device, using the same email address.

Messages includes these features:

- Supports iMessage, AIM (AOL Instant Messenger), Jabber, Google Talk, and Yahoo Messages accounts (Messages > Preferences > Accounts pane).

- Contacts integration.

- One-to-one or multiperson typed conversations.

- Delivery and read receipts (iMessage only).

- End-to-end encryption secures iMessage conversations.

- Search messages by text or recipient.

- Video and audio chat via FaceTime/iSight camera (or other webcam or microphone).

- Automatically find other Messages users on your local network.

- Background, image, and video effects.

- Multiple chats in a single window or in separate windows.

- Message forwarding (right-click selected messages and then choose Forward).

- Unified buddy list.

- Unified status.

- Buddy search.

- Screen-sharing for getting live help from other Mac users.

- Timestamped chat histories.

- Formatted text and smileys.

- File exchange (Buddies > Send File). iMessage allows attachments of up to 100MB.

- Send email (Buddies > Send Email).

Tip: To sync Messages with Gmail (Google Talk), Yahoo (Yahoo Messages), or other services that support messages, choose > System Preferences > Mail, Contacts & Calendars, select the account, and then turn on Messages.

Notes

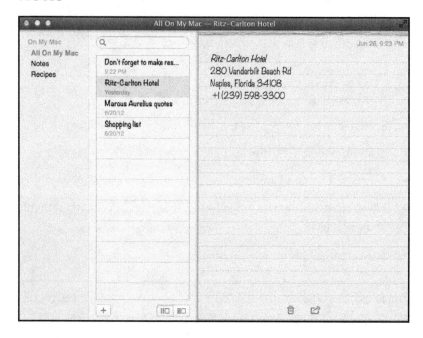

Use the Notes application to type notes on a virtual pad of scratch paper. It's also a handy place to paste text and photos copied from Safari, Mail, or other apps. Notes supports Auto Save, share sheets, and full-screen view.

Notes includes these features:

- To create a new note, choose File > New Note (Command+N) or click ➕.

  A list of notes appears on the left, and the current note is highlighted. Notes are listed chronologically, with the most recently modified note at the top. Each item in the list shows the first few words of the note.

- To view or edit a note, click it in the notes list.

- Paste or drag text, images, or web addresses (URLs) into notes.

- To format a note, select the target text and then use the Format menu. You can format a note with fonts, rich text, bulleted items, and numbered lists.

- To find a note, type or paste text in the Search box.

- To pin a note to the desktop, double-click it in the notes list. Pinned notes stay visible even when Notes is closed.

- To delete a note, right-click it in the notes list and then choose Delete, or click the Trash icon at the bottom of the note.

- You can organize notes in a hierarchy of folders. To view a list of folders, choose View > Show Folders List. To create a new folder, choose File > New Folder (Shift+Command+N). To view a folder's notes, click the folder in the folders list. To move a note to a different folder, drag the note from the notes list to the target folder. To nest folders, drag a folder onto another. To delete or rename a folder, right-click it in the folders list (deleting a folder also deletes its notes and subfolders).

- To use iCloud to sync notes wirelessly across your Macs and iOS devices, choose > System Preferences > iCloud > Notes. To set the default account for synced notes, in Notes, choose File > Default Account.

- To sync Notes with Gmail, Yahoo, or other services that support notes, choose > System Preferences > Mail, Contacts & Calendars, select the account, and then turn on Notes.

Reminders

The Reminders application lets you create and manage to-do lists. You can add reminders to custom lists, assign them to future due dates, receive notifications when they come due, and mark them as completed to hide them from view. You can create multiple to-do lists to keep your work, personal, and other tasks separate. Reminders comes with two lists: Reminders for active reminders and Completed for finished tasks. Reminders supports Auto Save.

Reminders includes these features:

• To view reminder lists, choose View > Show Sidebar or press Option+Command+S. To create a new list, choose File > New List (Command+L). To view a list's reminders, click the list in the sidebar. To move a reminder to a different list, drag the reminder to the target list or right-click it and then choose Move to List. To reorder lists, drag them up or down. To delete or rename a list, right-click it in the sidebar (deleting a list also deletes its reminders).

- To create a new reminder, click the target list and then choose File > New Reminder (Command+N) or click ⊞.

- To edit a reminder, right-click it and then choose Show Info, or click the reminder's *i* button, which appears when you point to a reminder. You can add a due date, set a priority, add a location-based (geofenced) alert, and more.

- To delete a reminder, right-click it and then choose Delete.

- To mark a reminder as completed, select its checkbox or right-click it and then choose Mark as Completed. Completed reminders are moved to the Completed list.

- To reorder reminders, drag them up or down.

- To pin a reminder list to the desktop, double-click it in the sidebar.

- To import or export reminders as **iCalendar** (.ics) files, use Import or Export commands in the File menu. iCalendar is a standard format that many email and calendar programs can read.

- To show a calendar in the sidebar, choose View > Show Calendar (Option+Command+K). Days with active reminders are marked with dots. To jump to today's date, choose View > Go to Today (Command+T).

- To use iCloud to sync reminders wirelessly across your Macs and iOS devices, choose > System Preferences > iCloud > Calendars & Reminders.

- To sync Reminders with Gmail, Yahoo, or other services that support reminders, choose > System Preferences > Mail, Contacts & Calendars, select the account, and then turn on Calendars & Reminders.

- To turn on notifications for reminders, choose > System Preferences > Notifications > Reminders.

Tip: Flick two fingers left or right on the trackpad to move quickly among reminder lists.

Share Sheets

A **share sheet** is a menu that appears when you click the Share button  or Share menu in an application that supports sharing. Share sheets let you share quickly and easily, with no need to switch apps or drag files. You can share via Mail, Messages, or AirDrop, or post straight to Twitter, Facebook, Vimeo, or Flickr (to sign in to your accounts, choose > System Preferences > Mail, Contacts & Calendars).

Depending on the app you're using, you can share text, documents, links, photos, or videos. In Safari, for example, you can share a webpage link via Mail, Messages, Facebook, or Twitter. In Notes, you can send a note by Mail or Messages. In Preview, the share button offers Mail, Messages, AirDrop, Facebook, Twitter, and Flickr. You can also share from Finder, Photo Booth, Contacts, iPhoto, QuickTime Player, and Quick Look. To share selected text from TextEdit, right-click the selection and then choose Share.

Twitter Integration

Twitter (*twitter.com*) is a popular third-party micro-blogging service that's available systemwide in OS X.

- To sign in to your Twitter account, choose > System Preferences > Mail, Contacts & Calendars > Twitter.

- You can send **tweets**—140-character messages—with attachments from several apps, including Safari, Preview, Photo Booth, iPhoto, TextEdit, and Quick Look. To tweet a link or photo, click the Share button 🔼 and then choose Twitter. To tweet selected text, right-click the selection and then choose Share > Twitter. While you're composing a tweet, the number at the bottom of the Tweet window shows the number of characters remaining that you can enter (up to 140). Attachments use some of a tweet's characters.

- To get notifications for direct messages and mentions, choose > System Preferences > Notifications > Twitter.

- Tweets can pick up your approximate location by using Location Services (choose > System Preferences > Security & Privacy > Privacy pane > Location Services).

- To add a Twitter field to a contact, open Contacts, select the contact, and then choose Card > Add Field > Twitter.

Facebook Integration

Note: Facebook integration is available in the Fall 2012 update of OS X.

Facebook (*facebook.com*) is a dominant social-networking service that's available systemwide in OS X.

- To sign in to your Facebook account, choose > System Preferences > Mail, Contacts & Calendars > Facebook.

- You can use share sheets to post photos, links, and comments straight to Facebook from Safari, Preview, Photo Booth, iPhoto, TextEdit, and Quick Look.

- To get Facebook notifications in Notification Center, choose >
  System Preferences > Notifications > Facebook. Click Options to
  specify which types of Facebook notifications to show (friend requests, comments, wall posts, and so on).

- Facebook posts can pick up your approximate location by using
  Location Services (choose > System Preferences > Security &
  Privacy > Privacy pane > Location Services). Click the location
  indicator in the Facebook share sheet to add a location to your post.

- Facebook friends appear in Contacts with profile photos and up-
  to-date information.

AirPlay Mirroring

You can use AirPlay, Apple's wireless file-streaming technology, to
mirror (duplicate) whatever is on your Mac's screen—videos, apps,
games, photos, presentations, websites, anything—to a high-definition
TV (HDTV), up to 1080p HD. You need an Apple TV (second genera-
tion or later) that's on the same wireless network as your Mac—OS X
detects the Apple TV automatically. Click the AirPlay icon on the
menu bar and select Apple TV to start mirroring. If the AirPlay icon
isn't visible, choose > System Preferences > Displays > Display pane >
"Show mirroring options in the menu bar when available".

AirPlay Mirroring scales your Mac's desktop image to fit your HDTV
screen. For a sharper image, set the resolution of your desktop to best
match that of your Apple TV. For privacy, signals between your Mac
and your Apple TV are encrypted.

Tip: AirPlay Mirroring sends audio (as well as video) from your Mac to your Apple
TV. You can use the audio feature independent of AirPlay Mirroring by selecting
your Apple TV in Sound preferences.

Software Updates via App Store

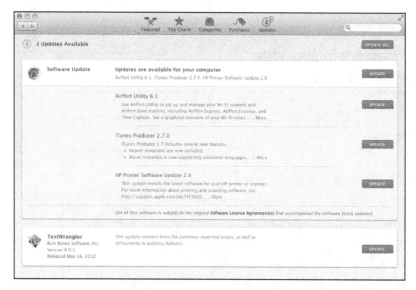

Apple regularly releases updates for OS X system software and other Apple programs. These updates include bug fixes, new features, security patches, version upgrades, and other improvements. All Apple software updates are available from the Updates section of the Mac App Store.

Tip: Updates for third-party programs downloaded from the App Store are also available from the App Store. If you didn't get a program from the App Store, check the developer's website for updates or use the program's built-in updater.

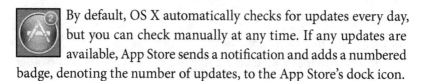 By default, OS X automatically checks for updates every day, but you can check manually at any time. If any updates are available, App Store sends a notification and adds a numbered badge, denoting the number of updates, to the App Store's dock icon.

To open App Store, choose > Software Update. Available updates are listed in the Updates pane. To learn more about an update, click its icon or its *More* link. You can update any single item by clicking Update next to its name, or you can update everything by clicking Update All at the top of the window. You're also free to ignore updates.

Tip: If you're on a large network, your network administrator might distribute updates via network server.

To set up Software Update:

Choose > System Preferences > Software Update.

Set the following options:

Automatically check for updates
  Check for updates automatically and periodically.

Download newly available updates in the background
  Download updates in the background without being asked. You'll still be notified before the updates are installed.

Install system data files and security updates
  Update and install critical system files without being asked.

Automatically download apps purchased on other Macs
  Download apps (from the Mac App Store) that you bought on other Macs.

Show Updates
  Open the Mac App Store and see any available updates.

Check Now
  Check for updates manually.

Power Nap

While your Mac sleeps, Power Nap will automatically:

* Download software updates from the App Store.

* Get the latest mail, notes, reminders, messages, calendar events, contact information, Photo Stream photos, and other iCloud updates.

* Make periodic Time Machine backups.

* Synchronize iCloud documents (Documents in the Cloud).

To turn on Power Nap, choose > System Preferences > Energy Saver > Battery pane > "Enable Power Nap while on battery power". For plugged-in Macs, you can configure Power Nap independently in the Power Adapter pane.

Power Nap works only on Macs that have flash memory, such as the MacBook Air (late 2010 or newer) or MacBook Pro with Retina display. If you have a compatible Mac but don't see Power Nap settings, you may have to update your firmware (> Software Update).

Power Nap works whether your Mac is plugged into a power outlet or is using battery power (draining little power). Power Nap refreshes the data on your Mac silently; no fans or lights come on and the display remains dark (but the drive, processor, and networking hardware are all active).

Deeper iCloud Integration

iCloud is an online storage and computing service that uploads (copies) your content to Apple's remote data center and pushes it wirelessly to your Mac, Windows PC, and iOS devices (iPhone, iPad, and iPod touch). Your music, photos, documents, and more are available on-demand across all your computers and iDevices. iCloud is integrated with your programs and works in the background silently and automatically (without manual syncing or sending). You can also view and manage your content and settings at *icloud.com* in a modern browser. Some iCloud features work across OS X, Windows, and iOS, whereas others are iOS-only.

A few iCloud tips:

• The minimal system requirements for iCloud are at "iCloud: Supported system requirements" (*support.apple.com/kb/HT4759*).

• iCloud provides unlimited free storage for purchased music, TV shows, iOS apps, and books. It also includes 5 GB of free storage for mail, documents, and backups. Higher storage capacities are available for an annual fee (*support.apple.com/kb/HT4874*). You can manage your storage by controlling backups and choosing which documents to store in the cloud (*support.apple.com/kb/HT4847*).

- iCloud identifies you by your Apple ID (*support.apple.com/kb/ HT4895*). Some iCloud features work across multiple Apple IDs (*support.apple.com/kb/TS4020*).

- iCloud stores your data securely. For details, read "iCloud: iCloud security and privacy overview" (*support.apple.com/kb/HT4865*).

To set up iCloud (OS X):

Choose > System Preferences > iCloud, enter your Apple ID and password (if prompted), and then select the services that you'd like to enable. The following services are available:

Mail

iCloud includes an *icloud.com* (formerly *me.com*) email account that keeps your mail and folders up-to-date across all your devices. For details, read "iCloud: Set up iCloud Mail on your devices and computers" (*support.apple.com/kb/PH2621*).

Contacts

Changes to your contacts in Contacts, iOS Contacts, and Microsoft Outlook 2007 or later are pushed automatically to iCloud across all your devices.

Calendars & Reminders

Changes to your calendars in Calendar, iOS Calendar, and Microsoft Outlook 2007 or later are pushed automatically to iCloud across all your devices, as are changes to your reminders in Reminders, iOS Reminders, and Microsoft Outlook 2007 or later. You can share your calendars with other iCloud users.

Notes

Changes to your notes in Notes and iOS Notes are pushed automatically to iCloud across all your devices.

Safari

Your Safari bookmarks, Reading List, and open tabs are pushed automatically to iCloud. In Windows, Safari and Internet Explorer bookmarks are pushed. To view synced tabs in Safari, click the iCloud button ☁ in the Safari toolbar.

Photo Stream

Photos imported to your Mac or Windows PC are automatically pushed to iCloud, as are photos taken on iOS devices. On your Mac, you can view the photos in iPhoto or Aperture. To enable Photo Stream, open iPhoto or Aperture, click the Photo Stream icon in the left sidebar, and then click Turn On Photo Stream. For details, read "iCloud: Photo Stream FAQ" (*support.apple.com/kb/HT4486*). You can also use Photo Stream photos as a screen saver (choose > System Preferences > Desktop & Screen Saver).

Documents & Data (Documents in the Cloud)

Transfer Pages, Keynote, and Numbers documents between your computer and your iOS devices. Sign in to *icloud.com/iwork* in a modern browser, and all your iWork for iOS documents will be there, complete with your most recent edits. You can also drag an iWork for Mac or Microsoft Office document (Word, PowerPoint, or Excel) from your computer to one of the iWork apps on *icloud. com*; it will appear automatically on all your iOS devices for viewing and editing. Third-party developers can make their apps work with iCloud, too. For details, read "iCloud: About using iWork for iOS and iCloud" (*support.apple.com/kb/HT4942*). If you can't update or upload documents to iCloud, read "iCloud: Troubleshooting Documents in the Cloud" (*support.apple.com/kb/TS3991*). You can also move documents to the cloud from Preview and TextEdit (File > Move To > iCloud).

Back to My Mac

Provides remote access to your Mac from another Mac anywhere on the internet. For details, read "OS X: Using and troubleshooting Back to My Mac with your iCloud account" (*support.apple.com/kb/ HT4907*).

Find My Mac

Helps locate a missing Mac. Sign in at *icloud.com* to see your missing Mac on a map. You can send a message, lock the Mac, or securely erase all its data.

To set up iCloud (Windows):

Download and install the iCloud Control Panel from Apple (*www.icloud. com/icloudcontrolpanel*). On the Windows desktop, choose Start > Control Panel > Network and Internet > iCloud, enter your Apple ID and password (if prompted), and then select the desired services.

To set up iCloud (iOS):

On the Home screen of your iPad, iPhone, or iPod touch, tap Settings > iCloud, enter your Apple ID and password (if prompted), and then turn on the desired services.

Other iCloud Services

Other iCloud services, not specific to OS X, include:

iTunes Match

A fee-based service that gives the benefits of iTunes in the Cloud for music you haven't bought from iTunes, including pirated music and music ripped from CDs. iTunes Match is built into iTunes on your Mac or Windows PC and the Music app on your iOS devices. You can download your entire music library from iCloud at any time.

Backup

iCloud automatically backs up important data on your iOS devices daily over wi-fi. Backups include purchased music, TV shows, apps, and books; photos and video in the Camera Roll; device settings; app data; home screen and app organization; messages (iMessage, SMS, and MMS); and ringtones. To restore a backup on your device (or set up a new device), connect the device to wi-fi, and then enter your Apple ID and password. Your backed-up data will appear on your device. For details, read "iCloud: How to back up iCloud data" (*support.apple.com/kb/HT4910*).

iTunes in the Cloud

Automatically downloads newly purchased iTunes music, iOS apps, and iBookstore books to all your iOS devices wirelessly over a wi-fi or cellular signal (previous purchases are downloaded at no charge). To enable automatic downloads, open iTunes on your Mac, and then choose iTunes > Preferences (Command+,) > Store pane > Automatic Downloads. In iTunes for Windows, choose Edit > Preferences (Control+,) > Store pane > Automatic Downloads. In iOS, on the Home screen, tap Settings > Store > Automatic Downloads.

Find My iPhone/iPad

Works like Find My Mac, but for iOS devices. To see your missing device on a map, sign in at *icloud.com* or use the Find My iPhone app (*itunes.apple.com/us/app/find-my-iphone/id376101648?mt=8*) on another iOS device.

Find My Friends

Use the Find My Friends app (*itunes.apple.com/us/app/find-my-friends/id466122094?mt=8*) to locate people. iOS users who share their location with you appear on a map. Privacy controls let you turn off location-sharing or share temporarily with a specific group of people. Parental restrictions let you manage how your children use Find My Friends.

Features for China

New features for Chinese speakers include:

- Chinese dictionary

- Baidu search in Safari

- QQ Mail, 163, and 126 services in Mail, Contacts & Calendars preferences

- New Chinese fonts

- Sina Weibo, Youku, and Tudou share sheets

- Improved Chinese keyboards and text input

Removed from Mountain Lion

The following programs and features have been removed or replaced:

- MobileMe has been replaced by iCloud

- Software Update has been replaced by App Store

- RSS support has been removed from Safari and Mail

- Notes has been removed from Mail (Notes is now a separate app)

- Java and X11 are now on-demand downloads

Index

www.ingramcontent.com/pod-product-compliance
Lightning Source LLC
LaVergne TN
LVHW052125070326
832902LV00038B/3939